# ANIMAL LIFESTYLES

# Climbers

## By Alison Ballance

## Table of Contents

Dominie Press, Inc.

# Introduction

For many people, climbing rocks and mountains is a fun thing to do. People need special **equipment** to be able to climb safely. Climbers wear special shoes with rubber **soles** that grip the rock. They use **harnesses** and safety ropes to protect them if they fall.

Many animals can climb much better than even the best rock climber. In this book, we will look at animals and plants that climb trees, rocks, and other things.

# Coconut Crabs

Even though coconut crabs are big and heavy, they are good climbers. They use their sharp claws to climb up coconut trees. The crabs knock coconuts out of the treetops, and then climb down to eat them on the ground.

*Coconut crabs are land crabs that live on islands in the Pacific Ocean, where they eat coconuts, plants, and dead animals. They can grow up to a foot long and weigh nine pounds.*

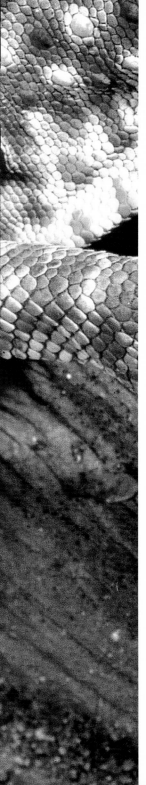

# Geckos

Geckos can walk up walls and across ceilings. They can even walk up a slippery **surface**, like glass. The soles of their feet are covered with millions of tiny hairs that stick to the surface like a **suction** cup. When the gecko wants to move, it peels its sticky feet off the wall.

*In tropical places, many geckos live inside people's houses. They hide during the day, and come out at night to eat insects that are attracted to the house lights.*

# Lemurs

Lemurs are related to monkeys and apes. They are very good at **leaping** between trees. They have long back legs to help them jump. Their hands have four fingers on one side and one long finger on the other side to help them **grasp** branches. The **palms** of a lemur's hands are soft for better gripping.

*Lemurs are found only in one place in the world: a big island called Madagascar.*

# Monkeys

Monkeys have strong grasping hands. They run through the **forest canopy**, leaping and swinging from branch to branch. Monkeys have good eyesight, so they can **judge** distances and heights.

*Like people, many monkeys have thumbs that help them grasp branches and food.*

11

# Cuscus

A cuscus is a kind of opossum. The back part of its tail is hairless and covered with **scales**. It can **wind** its tail around branches to help it climb.

A cuscus is a **marsupial**, which means the female carries her baby in a pouch on her stomach. A kangaroo is another type of marsupial.

*This kind of cuscus comes out at night to feed on fruit and leaves. A cuscus spends all its life in trees without ever going down to the ground.*

# Snakes

A snake does not have hands or feet – but it can still climb trees. It presses its body tightly against the tree trunk and **molds** it around bumps, hollows, and rough patches. It moves by rippling its body from its head all the way to the tip of its tail.

*Most snakes live in hot countries because they need the sun to keep warm and active.*

# Woodpeckers

A woodpecker spends a lot of time **darting** around tree trunks. It has short legs with two toes pointing forward and two toes pointing backward. A woodpecker's tail is very important, too. When it digs for insects in the wood, it **props** itself up with its tail – almost like having a third leg.

Woodpeckers build their nests by digging holes in trees. They do not search for nest material like other birds. They use the sawdust they made while digging the holes.

# Leopards

Leopards climb into trees to sleep or to eat their prey. They have hooked claws that dig into trees like the metal spikes that mountaineers put on their boots. When leopards walk on the ground, they **retract** their claws.

*A leopard is very strong. It can pull an animal that is much heavier than itself up into a tree.*

# Fig Trees

Did you know that plants can climb, too? Birds eat fig tree seeds and spread them through the forest in their droppings. The seeds often fall in cracks and holes high up in trees. They **sprout** long roots, which grow down the trunk of the big tree to reach the forest floor.

*The fig tree's roots wrap around the **host** tree it is growing on. The fig tree often grows so large that it kills the host tree. The fig's branches and roots keep standing, even when the host tree is gone.*

# Summary

Trees and rocks are good places to escape and hide from predators. Trees are also good places to find food, such as leaves, fruit, and insects.

Animals that climb trees have hands, feet, and tails that help them move quickly in the branches without falling. Some monkeys have long arms and a long tail that they can wrap around branches like a hand. They sometimes hang from branches by their tails so they can use both of their hands at the same time.

When people climb trees and rocks, we must use special equipment. We use ropes, harnesses, and ladders so we will not fall.

# Glossary

| | |
|---|---|
| **darting** | moving quickly |
| **equipment** | special tools needed to do something |
| **forest canopy** | the treetops |
| **grasp** | to hold on to something firmly |
| **harnesses** | special straps that a climber wears |
| **host** | a plant or animal that supports the life of another plant or animal |
| **judge** | to decide |
| **leaping** | jumping onto something |
| **marsupial** | mammals that carry their young in pouches |
| **molds** | fits something to the shape of a different object |
| **palms** | the flat parts of hands |
| **prey** | an animal that is hunted by another animal |
| **props** | supports by leaning on something |
| **retract** | to pull something out of the way |
| **scales** | small plates of skin that overlap each other |
| **soles** | the bottom parts of shoes or feet |
| **suction** | a special kind of grip |
| **surface** | outside area of an object |
| **sprout** | when a plant is beginning to grow |
| **wind** | to wrap around tightly |

# Index